COMMON OBJECTS OF LOVE

The annual Stob Lectures, normally devoted to the fields of ethics, apologetics, and philosophical theology, are presented each fall on the campus of Calvin College or Calvin Theological Seminary in honor of Henry J. Stob.

Dr. Stob, with degrees from Calvin College and Calvin Theological Seminary, Hartford Seminary, and the University of Göttingen, began his distinguished career as a professor of philosophy at Calvin College in 1939 and in 1952 was appointed to teach philosophical and moral theology at Calvin Theological Seminary, where he remained until retirement. He died in 1996, leaving many students influenced greatly by his teaching.

The Stob Lectures are funded by the Henry J. Stob Endowment and are administered by a committee including the presidents of Calvin College and Calvin Theological Seminary.

For more information on Dr. Stob and The Stob Lectures, see www.calvin.edu/stob.

COMMON OBJECTS OF LOVE

Moral Reflection and the Shaping of Community

• •

THE 2001 STOB LECTURES

Oliver O'Donovan

WILLIAM B. EERDMANS PUBLISHING COMPANY

GRAND RAPIDS, MICHIGAN / CAMBRIDGE, U.K.

Wm. B. Eerdmans Publishing Co.
255 Jefferson Ave. S.E., Grand Rapids, Michigan 49503 /
P.O. Box 163, Cambridge CB3 9PU U.K.

Printed in the United States of America

07 06 05 04 03 02   7 6 5 4 3 2 1

Library of Congress Cataloging-in-Publication Data

O'Donovan, Oliver.
Common objects of love : moral reflection and the shaping of
community : 2001 Stob lectures / Oliver O'Donovan.
         p.   cm.
Includes bibliographical references.
ISBN 0-8028-0515-9 (alk. paper)
1. Christian ethics. I. Title.
BJ1251 .O36 2002

241 — dc21

2002029489

www.eerdmans.com

CONTENTS

PREFACE

I have resisted the temptation to write up these Stob Lectures, delivered at Calvin College and Seminary in November 2001, into a real book. In this I hope I shall be thought to have done no disrespect either to my hosts or to the memory of Dr. Henry Stob, whose contribution to Calvin College is honored in the annual lecture series to which I was privileged to contribute. I would like, on the contrary, to pay respect to the lecture series in general as a real form of serious communication, and to that one instance of it in particular as an experience of real lecturing, not least by virtue of the quality of the discussion periods accompanying the lectures. If lectures are worth delivering and listening to and discussing, and if they form a suitable tribute to those who have set us examples of Christian thought and instruction, we need not, perhaps, be so ashamed of them as to turn them into something quite different before we let them loose on a wider public.

These three lectures in particular would be very difficult to turn into something else without destroying what they actually were. I conceived of them initially as a single train of thought which would unite some of the intellectual concerns of my hosts with some concerns of my own. But then, as a result of what transpired on September 11, 2001, they also became an opportunity for a first reflection upon the meaning of those traumatic events for our civilization. Their genesis is fixed very particularly in the history of our times, and they need to be read as an intellectual record of their own moment.

In expressing my special gratitude to the presidents of Calvin College and Calvin Seminary and to Calvin College's Department of Philosophy and my long-standing friend John Hare, I extend thanks to all the students and faculty who made my first visit to Calvin memorable and pleasurable. A word of tribute is also due to my friend and publisher Jon Pott, and to the distinguished house of William B. Eerdmans, another jewel in the crown of the city of Grand Rapids. The third lecture draws on material which first appeared as "The Concept of Publicity" in the journal *Studies in Christian Ethics* (2000), to the editor of which I am most grateful. My gratitude is also due to Michael Wykes of St. Peter's College, Oxford, who patiently and with great expedition undertook the preparation of the typescript.

Christ Church, Oxford

I

OBJECTS OF LOVE

The journey of thought that is undertaken in these lectures does not circle comfortably around its subject like a pleasant afternoon stroll, but sets out for a far country. From some lighthearted puzzles about practical reason, it will arrive at some distant heart-searchings about modern society, on the way traversing a varied terrain, sometimes speculative and philosophical, sometimes proclamatory and theological. To arm you against the occasional suspicion that your guide has lost his way, you should have an overall compass-bearing, and this is given by the title, *Common Objects of Love*. It is the question of what unifies a multitude of human agents into a community of action and experience sustained over time.

Into the midst of my preparation for The Stob Lectures there broke the events of September 11, giving it a sharp point.

The hostility which produced those results was said, and surely rightly, to be directed at Western civilization as a whole. Yet they evoked a heightened sensitivity to *national* identities. What the members of the Congress sang, as they gathered emotionally on Capitol Hill, was not "O God Our Help in Ages Past," but "God Bless America." What that means, and whether another, quite new logic of connection has supervened to make such traditional patriotism obsolescent, is something that no one who thinks about our age can avoid pondering. Above all, it demands to be considered in the light of faith by those who put their hope neither in their country nor in Western civilization, but in the coming of Jesus to judge the living and the dead.

I want to begin with two puzzles about my own professional task as a teacher of ethics. They arise from a traditional doctrine (it comes from Aristotle, but has many lives) that reason functions in two contrasting ways: as "theoretical" reason about what is the case, and as "practical" reason about what we are to do. According to this doctrine the conclusions of our reasoning, if successful, fall into two types: they are *truths*, or they are *decisions*. The truths may be timeless truths about order and rationality or contingent truths about events; but either way they will be independent of ourselves, for we simply *know* them. The decisions, on the other hand, are not independent of ourselves; they are our input into the world's events. The propositions which express these two kinds of conclusion will be "descriptive" or "prescriptive"; that is to say, they will contain words like "is" and "are" and "did," on the one hand, words like "good," "right," and "ought," on the other.

Now, when I teach ethics, on this account, I am teaching how to think about how to act; and in teaching *Christian* ethics I am teaching how to think from truths of Christian faith to conclusions in Christian action. Ethics is not directly practical instruction, like car maintenance or computer programming; but it is practical indirectly, in that it communicates truths that govern action, such as that God created marriage as a life-long union of man and woman, and it teaches formal disciplines of decision, such as that we may not make exceptions in our own interest. So far the familiar theory — "Aristotelian," we call it, without being too punctilious about what Aristotle himself actually said.

Now for the first puzzle: Much of the subject matter of the ethical curriculum issues in decisions that no student of mine is likely to make, so that my teaching it appears to be a prodigal waste. This is especially true of political ethics, in which I have tended to specialize. If I teach sexual ethics, I may score high on applicability, provided that I keep to the most common questions. But if I teach the ethics of war, I am likely to score low. Most discussions of public policy will end in decisions with which ordinary citizens have nothing to do: Should we have an offensive or a defensive nuclear shield? Should we be prepared to defend national economic interests at the price of war? Should we invest in countries with inhuman labor policies? These decisions belong to strategists, politicians, and corporate bankers, not to us. What is the use of studying them in the context of a general moral education?

This puzzle may not at first seem very severe. Our instinct is to suppose that an understanding of such deliberations *must* be useful somehow, even though we may not face these decisions ourselves directly. Though the statistical probability is small, anyone *may* face them; and they are so important that it is worth a little waste to ensure that those who do face them have had the opportunity to think about them. Or, again, decision-makers need advisors, and an education in ethics ensures a plentiful supply of "ethical consultants," that ubiquitous new shoot on the capitalist trunk. We may then go on to claim that since decisions of different kinds interlock with one another, even those who do not face them directly as decision-makers or advisors may face them indirectly in the context of other decisions, as small investors, perhaps. But in any case, we will conclude with mounting confidence, this is a democracy, where we have to think about such questions anyway in order to vote.

With this last claim we come to an important focal point, which will engage us further. In the form in which it springs to our lips as part of the democratic vernacular, it is obviously untrue, since it assumes a romantic and unreal picture of democracy. It is not, in fact, the case that voters are asked to resolve these questions, but only to decide on who is to represent them in deliberative assemblies which will resolve them; and their usual fate is to face a field of candidates none of whom appears capable of thinking or talking coherently about them. Democracy would have to be very different from what it is, if voters needed to deliberate upon such practical questions more carefully than their representatives do. But suppose we lower the pitch of our claim for democratic institutions. We may say, it is a *contextual* condition for responsible decision-making in government that these deliberations should be shared as widely and intelligently as possible in the public arena. Popular debate provides a kind of acoustic ambience for political decision-making; the more sympathetic the ambience, the better the decisions that will be made. This seems to me to be a believable account of how public debate contributes to government, though it is not confined to democracies but applies to any well-ordered "politic" regime.

But it creates a difficulty for the Aristotelian doctrine from which we started. For if all our reasoning is either *about* fact or *toward* decision, to which category of reasoning does this ambient deliberation belong? Our puzzle about wasted educational effort has now reformulated itself as a puzzle about collective deliberation. How can we understand a political form of practical reasoning, where all contribute to the thinking but only a few make the decisions?

This new perspective on our puzzle follows from relying on our first instinct, that studying such political questions must be useful. But it is worth considering how we may defend moral education if we cease to rely on it. Introduce the familiar difference between educational value and useful training. Learning about political decisions may have no direct usefulness, we may say, in the sense of preparing us to make those same decisions, but it does have a considerable educational value. Indeed, precisely the fact that students are not likely to be faced with decisions about whether to become soldiers makes this a preeminently suitable pedagogical exercise. If the student is asked to discuss sex the whole time, the natural anxieties born of self-consciousness can inhibit learning and distort the capacity for clear-headed thought. We need topics on which we have some distance in order to learn the disciplines of moral deliberation.

This strategy appeals to a principle that every educator understands: there is pedagogical strength in emotional distance. Yet it hardly seems to meet the case here. It is, after all, notorious that people, especially young people, become deeply involved in political causes. Talk to any of the demonstrators at Genoa in July, and you would be more likely, I wager, to get a cool and lucid discourse on sex than on politics. So this attempt to resolve the puzzle brings us back again to the mystery of political identification. Political ethics is not in fact what it seems that it ought to be, a realm of detached and distanced school exercises. On the contrary, it is a warren of hidden sympathies and covert identifications, which break cover disconcertingly in alien and unexpected commitments. But how does this happen? How is it that, as the Gilbert and Sullivan song said, "every boy and every gal that's born into the world alive is either a little Liberal or else a little Conservative"? Nothing in the Aristotelian doctrine, we may say, prepared us for it, or can help us understand it.

So much for the first puzzle, which turned on the value of teaching political ethics and led us to the mystery of political collectives. But I warned you that I had two puzzles about the Aristotelian doctrine and the teaching of ethics. The second concerns decisions *in the past:* how is it that we appear to engage in deliberations that are *already concluded?* This is not a puzzle for academic ethics alone. If the verbs "ought to" and "ought not to" are supposed to conclude a train of practical reasoning, what of those same verbs accompanied by past infinitives: "ought to have" and "ought not to have," phrases by no means overheard only in classrooms, but prolific in everyday speech? What is their function? They can hardly express an actual moral decision. We cannot decide *now* whether to enter the Second World War; yet we continue to argue insatiably whether Britain *ought to have* declared war a year earlier, whether the United States *ought to have* avoided entering at all, etc. What is it that we are trying to resolve?

It is possible to entertain — as I once did — a pedagogical explanation of this puzzle, too. To ask about what *ought to have* been done, I thought, was to project ourselves imaginatively into a historical situation and to make the decision again, rather like an art student copying a masterpiece. The purpose was that of any hypothetical exercise: to learn, by abstracting from the historical facticity of the actual decision, the principles and disciplines that pertained to it, and that ought to govern us in any *future* decisions of the same kind we might happen to face.[1] So the judgment, "If he had survived Little Bighorn, Custer should have been court-martialled," was a

1. I expressed this view in "How Can Theology Be Moral?" *Journal of Religious Ethics* XVII (1989), p. 83.

kind of shorthand for, "Commanders who behave as Custer did at Little Bighorn should be court-martialled."

Now, it is true that historical cases provide helpful hypothetical exercises, and that the moral imagination thrives on hypothetical exercises in general. But as an account of what we commonly mean by the phrases "ought to have" or "ought not to have," this seems strained and artificial. Think of the reproaches we inflict upon ourselves immediately when we are conscious of having said or done something wrong: "Damn it! I shouldn't have mentioned that I voted for the Labour Party!" Such remorse is not about what I should *now* do, or should do *in future*, but precisely about what I *have* done. The artificial account is forced on us by the supposition that "ought" is a word by which we uniquely express decisions.

—⁓—

The goal of this long preamble has been to unsettle the Aristotelian doctrine about the two kinds of reasoning, and to prepare the way for a correction to it. I need hardly say that this ambition is not an original one. The sense that there must be something "behind" the distinction of theoretical and practical reason has been alive in Western thought wherever there has been a memory of the Platonic doctrine of the unity of being and the good. In the ancient world the Platonic tradition propounded a threefold rather than a twofold division of reason: besides logic, which was about what could be asserted, and ethics, which was about what could be done, there was also "physics" (metaphysics, in our terms) about what truly was. In our own generation there have been some stimulating proposals along these lines, of which I mention merely one. The German philosopher Robert Spaemann speaks of an "existential reason," which is both practical and theoretical. The reality that we grasp existentially, Spaemann thinks, is the *other person*, who is at once our door to ontology and to ethics. Personal being is what we understand by "being" before anything else. To grasp the reality of the other person is to grasp that there is a reality apart from ourself; so the other person is a "universal horizon." The "value" of the other person is not a *second* quality alongside the "reality" of the other person; there is an "indefinable simple quality," both ontological and ethical, an *Urphänomen*, which we call "dignity."[2] Reason grasps this not in *two* ways, believing the truth of it on the one hand and deciding obediently on the other, but in one way, which Spaemann calls both "attention" and "benevolence."

I mention Spaemann's middle way between practical and theoretical reason for its fascination and importance, and to

2. "Über den Begriff der Menschenwürde," in *Grenzen* (Stuttgart: Klett-Cotta, 2001), p. 109.

indicate that we are here treading ground that others have traversed extensively. But his appeal to the category of "person" is not essential to our purposes here. Our own needs can be met more economically with a proposition, derived from St. Augustine, that we know only as we love. Knowledge, which participates in the eternal Word of God, is consubstantial and coeternal with the Love that is God's eternal Spirit. All knowledge, then, has an affective aspect, just as all love has a cognitive aspect. Our experience of knowing is that of discerning good and welcoming it *as* good. To know any thing is to grasp its inherent intelligibility, which is its good; but to grasp its intelligibility is to grasp *it*, and, in grasping it, to cling to it in love. Let me explore this doctrine further by way of three comments:

(a) In proposing a knowledge prior to the separation of theoretical and practical reason, it conceives of it as a union of the two, a *both-and*, rather than a *tertium quid*. Practical and theoretical reason are each one-sided elaborations of a primary affective knowledge.

For reason to be "theoretical," in the sense of concerning itself wholly with the truth of things, it must abstract, hypothetically, from the loving orientation to reality that is really the condition of our knowledge. "Disinterested" knowledge, in other words, such as has been cultivated especially within the natural sciences, is not a primordial posture of knowledge, but an artifice, a sophisticated technique of enquiry. To detach oneself and one's interests from events into which one enquires, to assume the posture of an impartial researcher, clambering into an eyrie of observation where one renounces all interest in affecting the course of events, that is an achievement of civilization, borrowed, we should note, by the sciences from the political skill of judgment. Solomon and the two women[3] is a paradigm not only for juridical discernment, but for every kind of experimental enquiry.

But precisely such abstraction of observer from event is a *practical* posture. We may be disinterested; but our disinterest is never disinterested. It is a posture cultivated in the service of a single interest, that of eliciting the truth out of ambiguity. A supreme interest in disclosing hidden truth is the condition for every disinterest in what may transpire under the microscope, or under cross-examination before the judge's bench. It is for that reason that scientific investigation has its own proper dignity, and makes certain *moral* claims upon our respect and participation. If the Aristotelian theory that dichotomized reason from the ground up were true, there

3. I Kings 3:16-28.

could be no practical dignity in disinterested enquiry. It would simply be a primordial form of knowing. But because this achievement is shot through with a moral commitment, a love of truth strong enough to sustain serious scientific virtues, it demands our responding love and respect.

(b) Equally, however, "practical reason," which carries us through to decision, is an abstraction. "Thinking morally" is a much wider activity than thinking toward decision. It includes an attention to the world which is both affective and evaluative, "existential," in Spaemann's term. Our whole world of beings and events is known to us only as we love and hate. At the root of moral thought is a necessary taking-stock of the world, a discrimination prior to any decision we may subsequently make to influence the world. We shall call this taking-stock "moral reflection," to distinguish it from moral *deliberation*, which is directed toward decision. The metaphors contained in these two words suggest the distinction: "reflection" is "turning back" to look on something that is already *there*, an existing reality, "behind you," as it were; "deliberation" is "weighing up," facing an alternative, looking at possible courses of action that have not yet occurred. This distinction underlies the famous difference between value-words and obligation-words in ethics, between the "good" and the "ought."

"Ought," "right," and so on are the vocabulary of deliberation; "good," "fine," and "beautiful" are the vocabulary of moral reflection.

Moral reflection is not without a practical significance, but it is not oriented to any *action* in particular, but to the task of existence itself. In reflection we answer the question "how shall we live?" not "what shall we do?" And these are different questions. The first is not merely a generalized summary of the second. It asks about our placement in the world, our relation to other realities. And by answering this kind of question we are not merely accumulating a store of provisional orientations that can be called on later in the event that some decision requires them. We are determining ourselves as fellow occupants of the universe. In a language that is as common as it is unhelpful, we are shaping our "identities." Actually, an "identity" is not something we shape, but is given us by God, prior to any existential reflection of our own. But what *becomes* of our identities is the result of moral discrimination, by which we understand and confirm ourselves as God has given us to ourselves — or, of course, refuse to. By relating ourselves cognitively and affectively to the good and evil that we see within the created world around us, we adopt a posture that is the source of all our actions, but is not itself another action, or a summary of actions, but an affirmation of what we are.

(c) The term by which the Augustinian tradition expressed the idea of an originally committed attention is "love." "Love" is importantly distinct from the way we use the term "will," a difference sometimes obscured by the fact that Augustine himself identified love and will, as did many subsequent Augustinians. But whereas the medieval Augustinian tradition took a decisively voluntarist turn, making will the dominant partner in the conjunction, Augustine understood willing as an aspect of loving. What is the difference we need to mark here?

Will has to do with decisions, punctiliar and immediate, elections between courses of action. We speak of "acts" of will, though in fact our willing to perform an act does not have to be a *distinct* act from the act we are willing to perform. I can go to the United States willingly, without having to do *two* things: first will to go, then go. On the other hand, I can will to go and then not go; and sometimes I can will to go with such a dramatic access of self-consciousness, like Hercules at the crossroads, that my willing stands out on its own as an event apart. Yet one way or the other willing is acting. The "act" of will is the "act" of the human being considered as the outcome of a deliberation.

Love, on the other hand, carries no *direct* implication of action. Christians heedful of St. John remember, of course, that love is attested by action: "let us not love in word or speech but in deed and in truth."[4] Inactive or idle love is illusory. But love is not *the same thing as* act, as will is. Love, rather, is an attitudinal disposition which gives rise to various actions without being wholly accounted for by any of them. The object of love is not an act of our own, but simply — to use an Augustinian phrase again — the "enjoyment" of its object; and "enjoyment" is not the name of something we do, but of a relation in which we stand. In enjoyment, the object is simply "there for us," which is what makes the difference between enjoyment and "use," where the object is put to the service of some project. Love, whatever actions it gives rise to, is contemplative in itself, rejoicing in the fact that its object is there, not wanting to do anything "with" it. And so love can be described in passive terms, as in Augustine's famous metaphor: "My weight is my love, by which I am drawn in whatever direction I go. . . ."[5]

———꩜———

How does this Augustinian perspective help us with the puzzles about moral reason from which we began? These were, you recall, in the first place, the puzzle of *collective* reasoning, the fact that communities can discuss at large matters on which only a few of them will make decisions; and in the second

4. 1 John 3:18.
5. *Confessions* 13.9.10.

16

place, the puzzle of reasoning about *history*, which deals with matters no one will decide on again, since the decisions were taken long ago.

We are now in a position to give a quick and obvious answer, an answer that might conclude the argument of these lectures rather earlier than envisaged. We can say quite simply that the puzzles were created solely by the prejudice that moral thinking had to end in making a decision, and that having freed ourselves from that prejudice, we need find these forms of moral reflection puzzling no longer. What we engage in when we discuss public policy, or when we discuss decisions made in past generations, is not moral deliberation at all, but what we have called "moral reflection." By it we discern "what is good and acceptable and perfect," as St. Paul exhorted us to do, not with a view to doing something, but for its own sake.[6] And since there is nothing in heaven or earth more worth knowing than what is good and acceptable and perfect, the whole enterprise needs no further justification. At which we could sound a final triumphant flourish about the *sovereign uselessness* of moral reflection. To be "useless" is the prerogative of those very few ultimate and wholly determinative things which are important to us as such, not because they acquire importance from some wider strategy.

6. Romans 12:2.

17

I shall not, however, sound this flourish. That quick and obvious answer has not yet got to the bottom of those interesting and puzzling forms of moral reasoning from which we began. The most important things they have to reveal to us still lie ahead. And if we wonder how anything can still lie ahead once we have found our way to that sovereign good which is valuable for its own sake and not for its consequences, we reply: those very things that are sovereignly useless are, by that same token, supremely useful. The fact that their importance to us derives from the importance of nothing else is the obverse of the fact that the importance of other things derives from their importance. So although there is no further back we can go in seeking a ground for them, there is a great deal further forward we can come in exploring how they ground other more immediately perceptible goods. The truth that God can be loved only for his own goodness and not for the sake of any other thing is only *apparently* inconsistent with the observation that there are many benefits in loving God. These benefits are not the reason why God is good; but God's goodness is the reason why there are these benefits, classically called (in the West) "effects" or (in the East) "energies" of God's goodness. God's goodness bears upon us in many ways and in many circumstances, and to love God for the sake of his goodness is also to love the ways in which his goodness is known to us.

It is the same with our moral reflection: we cannot stop short at finding it good in itself; we must see how it generates and supports useful goods of deliberative thought toward action. Those goods are precisely the goods of communal deliberation and of deliberation about the past, which on first appearance struck us as paradoxical. We can save the face of these deliberations and show that they actually make sense as such, rather than merely reclassify them as reflection. It is not, after all, a mere illusion that we seem to deliberate corporately or to deliberate in respect of past actions.

The new factor introduced into the analysis of moral reasoning is this: from its reflective roots to its deliberative fruits moral reasoning is a shared and collective enterprise, not a private and individual one. Loving, like knowing, is something we do only with others. Together, not alone, we acquire our capacity to engage the world in cognitive affection. The goods that we love, created and uncreated, are goods common to all, and we love them properly as our own goods only as we understand that they are everybody else's. Simply in loving them, we become part of a community that is not constructed to accomplish some task but is given in the very fact that we cannot but love them. Because this is true of the reflective roots of moral reason, it is true of our deliberations, too. The original form of the question about action is, "What shall *we* do?" "We" are the community of human agents. Only secondarily, and in the pursuit of casuistic particularity, do we elaborate the "we" question into the distinct questions "What shall I do?" "What shall you do?" "What shall they do?"

In the next two chapters we shall explore the connection between love and community. In doing this we shall call to our aid another doctrine from Augustine, perhaps, after his notorious speculations about predestination, his most controversial single contribution to Western thought. It concerns the definition of a "people":

> A people, we may say, is a gathered multitude of rational beings united by agreeing to share the things they love. There can be as many different kinds of people as there are different things for them to love. Whatever those things may be, there is no absurdity in calling it a people if it is a gathered multitude, not of beasts but of rational creatures, united by agreeing to share what they love. The better the things, the better the people; the worse the things, the worse their agreement to share them.[7]

7. Augustine *City of God* 19.24. *Populus est coetus multitudinis rationalis rerum quas diligit concordi communione sociatus, profecto, ut uideatur qualis quisque populus sit, illa sunt intuenda, quae diligit. Quaecumque tamen diligat, si coetus est multitudinis non pecorum, sed rationalium creaturarum et eorum quae diligit*

This imitated and amended a definition from Cicero that a people was a multitude "united in association by a common sense of right and a community of interest," replacing a reference to "law and common interest" with the phrase "common objects of love." Augustine's purpose, it is often said, though not uncontroversially, was to challenge an idealist understanding of organized social life with a realist one. To expect "law" of a political entity was to expect too much, Augustine thought. If one only understood what a high and comprehensive good law really was, the most that one could reasonably expect of sinful and prideful communities was some consensus on goals worth pursuing. My purpose is not to reexplore the disagreement between idealism and realism, nor to arbitrate on the interpretative controversy about where Augustine came down. I want simply to explore the idea that moral reflection, the identification of objects of love, has effect *in organized community.* The value of the reflective enterprise is seen in the corporate shape that it confers on our collectives, in the creative miracle that by sharing a common view of the good, we become a "multitude" no longer, but a "people," capable of common ac-

---

concordi communione sociatus est, non absurde populus nuncupatur; tanto utique melior, quanto in melioribus, tantoque deterior, quanto est in deterioribus concors. Translation in *From Irenaeus to Grotius: A Sourcebook in Christian Political Thought,* ed. O. O'Donovan & J. Lockwood O'Donovan (Grand Rapids: Eerdmans, 1999), p. 162.

tion, susceptible to common suffering, participating in a common identity.

When we speak with Augustine of "love," there is nothing idealistic in the word. We have not leaped with one bound to that love which "bears all things, believes all things," and "never fails."[8] To invoke *that* love prematurely has often been a temptation in Christian reflection on society, signaling a drift toward the sentimental, a forgetfulness of the sting of sin. For Augustine the love that forms communities is undetermined with respect to its object, and so also undetermined with respect to its moral quality: "the better the things, the better the people; the worse the things, the worse their agreement to share them."[9] Furthermore, every determination of love implies a corresponding hatred. For a community to focus its love on *this* constellation of goods is to withdraw its love from *that*. Every concrete community, then, is defined equally by the things it does *not* love together, the objects it refuses to accept as a ground of its association. So it is that the two ultimate communities, the "two cities" in which all human beings are grouped, are determined not only by ultimate objects of love, but by ultimate objects of refusal: "love of God to the point of

8. 1 Corinthians 13:7.
9. *City of God* 19.24.

22

contempt of self, love of self to the point of contempt of God."[10]

Yet this element of indeterminacy does not mean that the objects of community-forming love are a matter of open choice. For the underlying unity of knowledge and love means that love can take form only as a cognizance of reality, adequate or inadequate. There is an objective measure by which we may differentiate "better" from "worse" loves, which is the adequacy of their grasp of reality. The loves of some communities attach to concrete material goods as their final term, while the loves of others treat those material goods as mediations of spiritual realities. Materialism, for Augustine, is the paradigm of the lying love, attached to real goods and yet untrue, since it misconceives the significance of those goods within reality as a whole. A view of politics as a choice between economic systems for distributing material goods would strike Augustine as a choice between two roads to Hell.

Furthermore, the unity of knowledge and love reflects, for Augustine, the image of the divine Trinity, in which the Word and the Spirit are consubstantial and coeternal. When we love some thing, however badly, it is a sign within our created being that we were made by God for God, in the order of the divine

10. *City of God* 14.28.

Word and the power of the divine Spirit. Our variously ignoble loves are not simply different from the love which bears all things and believes all things; nor is it wrong to take the content of that holy love as the measure of the challenge that God has set for our communal loves. Secular social reality, we may say, is constantly subverted by a conspiracy of nature and grace. The community-building love that the Creator has set in all human hearts, and that makes even Hell a city, will always need redemptive love if it is to realize its own capacities. Secular community has no ground of its own on which it may simply exist apart. It is either opened up to its fulfillment in God's love, or it is shut down, as its purchase on reality drains relentlessly away.

2

AGREEMENT TO SHARE

Thus far, we have been led from some puzzles about deliberation to contemplate two connected truths. The first
was that moral thought not only runs forward, as it were, toward the decisions that convert it into action, but runs back-
ward to establish our elementary knowledge of the world as a
kind of love. The second was that this loving knowledge of the
world is the ground on which we deliberate and act not only as
individuals, but as communities. My aim now is to explore
how community in general, and political society in particular,
arise out of the love of good things, still taking as my guide
Augustine's definition of a people as "a gathered multitude of
rational beings united by agreeing to share the things they
love." Augustine's interest was focused, as ours will be, upon
how community has its root in evaluations that we form and

hold together, the *common objects of love*. Loving is the corporate function that determines and defines the structure of the political society; it is the key to its coherence and its organization. Loving *things*, not loving *one another*. Augustine also affirmed that members of a community loved one another; but that is a second step. The love that founds the community is not reciprocal, but turned outward upon an object.

From this point forward our exploration falls into two phases. In the first I shall sketch an account of how communities mediate love and knowledge. This will be familiar enough as belonging to the idealist tradition, and is the kind of account that has enjoyed a revival under the "communitarian" influence of figures such as Alasdair MacIntyre. In the second phase I shall disturb the serene calm of this picture by confronting it with plurality, error, and sin, and shall ask how it may be reconfigured in an evangelical context.

"Community" means a sphere in which things are held in common rather than in private, as "ours" rather than as "yours" or "mine." The essence of community is "communication," the exercise of sharing things or transmitting them among two or more people. The Greek noun *koinōnia*, St. Paul's designation for the holy society of the church, has a *verbal* sense ("sharing," as in 1 Corinthians 10:16) as well as a *concrete* sense ("a fellowship," as in 1 Corinthians 1:9), and this verbal sense continued to be felt in the Latin Christian tradition of the West, where the medieval scholastics used to render it in Latin not only as *communitas* but as *communicatio*. Those who are partners to communication (*koinonia* in the verbal sense) form a community (*koinonia* in the concrete sense). They become a "we" in relation to the object, whatever it is, that is common to them.

In its original sense one could speak of "communicating" any kind of good, material or spiritual. Our modern habit of confining the term to transmissions of a semantic order — to words, gestures, and electronic signals — seems something of an unnecessary restriction. Yet there is a true perception behind it. For at the center of all human communication is *the word*, the paradigm of all shared objects, the only object that is *essentially* shared, never divisible into private lots, but capable of being used only for communication. Other animal species display a variety of ways of being social: herding, for defense; coupling, for breeding; nursing, for the rearing of young; cooperative hunting; and so on. Yet we hesitate to speak of any of these as forming a "community," since they lack, we presume, a reflexivity, a consciousness of what is going on. That reflexivity is conferred upon us by the use of speech. Words have the capacity to organize and interpret other things noetically; they are the primary signs by which we invest other things with significations. "Between men and beasts," said Hooker, "there is no possibility of social communion, because the wellspring of that communion is a natural delight which man hath to trans-fuse from himself into others, and to receive from others into himself especially those things wherein the excellency of his kind doth most consist."[11]

The defining question of politics, then — what is the human mode of association? — is answered by pointing to the power of signification. A species that relates to its goods through appetite alone may or may not be social, but a species that relates to its goods through signs can only be a sharing species. Human com-munication is achieved by discourse that invests all other goods with cultural meaning; it involves not merely a common use of material goods but a common understanding of their signifi-cance. Out of the simplest material communications, then, it weaves complex cultural communications. What among herding animals is simply the peaceful sharing of forage, among humans becomes a shared meal: a sign of friendship, an affirmation of shared purpose, a pledge of loyalty, and many other things.

Together with shared understanding of objects, there arises an understanding of ourselves, the sharers. Common objects of love generate common self-understanding. This is assisted by a special kind of signification, which extracts from

11. Richard Hooker *Laws of Ecclesiastical Polity* 1.10.12.

the universe of objects some that will assume a representative meaning and will stand concretely for the sphere of communication itself. Some object or person presents our community to us, so that we bring within the scope of our perception what cannot be perceived directly as such, but only inferred, the totality of our own communications. To this object or person we direct the love that arises with our self-knowledge, a love that would, without a concrete object, be too diffuse to sustain. We call this special kind of signification "representation."

It is seen at its clearest in the special case of political representation. Here a society envisages its capacity to act together and as a whole through the actions of one person. The need to envisage the abstraction of our common action concretely enough ensures a quasi-monarchical aspect to political representation, even though monarchy can never be more than an appearance, since the practical exigencies of government demand, even in the simplest societies, the coordinated activity of an elite class. An intelligent Martian reading one of our more sophisticated political journals — say, *The Economist* of London — would be unlikely to learn that the government of any nation on Earth was in the hands of more than one person: "Mr. Bush intends this, Mr. Blair does that, and Mr. Putin plans the following" — all apparently acting alone and without associates! It is not for nothing that the president of the United States is constantly referred to, without a trace of irony, as "the most powerful person in the world"! Yet it is only a representation.

I am interested here, however, not so much in the special case of political representation as in the general practice. Political representation depends intricately upon a system of social representations. In the anointing of a political representative there converges a range of symbols that represent various strands of society — and this, rather than a debate on policy, is the true function of the electoral campaign in modern democracy. Concrete objects are pressed into service to represent society. To take the simplest example: the traveler long absent from home turns his thoughts and his affections toward some concrete thing connected with his homeland — a grain elevator, a dairy herd, a skyscraper, or whatever, and this represents his community to him, quite irrespective of whether he has eaten the bread made from that grain, drunk the milk from that herd, or occupied a desk in that building. When the desolate psalmist had to speak of the cultural and political destruction of God's elect people, he conceived that loss of collective identity as the loss of certain representative visible objects: "We see not our own signs."[12] What were these? Probably the temple and its sanctuary; but to him they were "our signs," attacked

12. Psalm 73:9.

and overwhelmed by the "signs" of the adversary, the military standards by which they made their presence known.

Through the mediation of representative signs, then, members of a community conceive of their community as such; they are recognizable to one another, and they attract one another's love. These are the means by which a community attains coherence. For it knows and loves itself as a kind of whole, a self-contained totality that embraces its members' various communications. Its self-love, therefore, is an organizing function within its understanding of the world, a decisive key to the evaluations it shares among its members. It interprets the order and rhythm of the cosmos and the nature and destiny of humankind. In the conception of "holy" things and places we can observe this confluence of political and cosmological meanings. What is holy in ancient Israel — the Sabbath, the temple, the land — at once organizes and structures the people as a political society and discloses the universal divine purpose for the world.

In this reflective movement a community is more than a sphere of sharing. It is what we call a "society," the object, to use a phrase of Erich Voegelin, of "transcendental representation."[13] Not all "common objects of love" are transcendental

13. For the association of Voegelin's transcendental representation with Augustine's common objects of love, see John von Heyking, *Augustine and Pol-*

representations, for society shares a range of material goods and understandings which bear none of this special burden of meaning. But these form the communal self-understanding, which structures all other shared meanings. They include representative objects, representative persons, representative histories, and representative ideas. They express what the society is, and they express what it is good for; they are forms of that knowledge of itself which is at the same time love of itself. They constitute the central core of the society's common way of seeing the world and living in it. And because the existence of a society is not atemporal, they constitute the core of its continuing identity in time, providing intelligible connections between past and present. In this function we refer to them as the "tradition" of the society.

The word "tradition," like *koinonia,* refers both to an action and a possession. In the first sense it is the activity by which one shares in the community, receiving and contributing. In the second sense it is the reserve of practices and communicative patterns received from the past — but only those which *continue* to command recognition, that is, which have been *effectively* communicated down to the present time. The essential thing about tradition is that it creates social continuity. It

---

itics as Longing in the World (Columbia: University of Missouri Press, 2001), pp. 77-109.

binds the communal action of the present moment to the communal actions of past moments. What we often call "traditionalism," the revival of lapsed traditions, is, properly speaking, a kind of innovation, making a new beginning out of an old model. This may or may not be sensible in any given instance, but it is not tradition. The claim of tradition is not the claim of the past over the present, but the claim of the present to that continuity with the past which enables common action to be conceived and executed.

The paradigm command of tradition is, "Honor your father and your mother, that your days may be long in the land which the LORD your God gives you."[14] It appears to our eyes to be concerned with the duties of children, but this is a mistake. The duties of children are purely responsive to the duty of parents to be to their children what *their* parents were to them. This is a command addressed to adults, whose existence in the world is not self-posited but the fruit of an act of cultural transmission, which they have a duty to sustain. The act of transmission puts us all in the place of receiver and communicator at once. The household is envisaged as the primary unit of cultural transmission, the "father and the mother" as representing every existing social practice which it is impor-

14. Exodus 20:12.

tant to carry on. Only so can community sustain itself within its environment, "the land which the LORD your God gives you." No social survival in any land can be imagined without a stable cultural environment across generations. By tradition society identifies itself from one historical moment to the next, and so continues to act as itself.

Of various means by which societies develop their transcendental representations I want *en passant* to notice two. The first is the narration of history. No educational or intellectual activity is more obviously tradition-bearing or more immediately associated with the representations of the community. Societies study their own history first and chiefly, even in academic life, typically promiscuous, while at the sub-academic level love of one's own is unrelieved. Those daily recorders of history whom we call "journalists" need no persuading about the preeminence of the local. In these ways we acknowledge that history fashions political self-awareness, for in telling our history we determine the terms on which we are to act as a community.

One of the puzzles about practical reason from which we began was how it is possible to think about what *should have been* done. This cannot be deliberation in a straightforward sense, as though we could make the decision of the past once again. We can only reflect on history, not deliberate about it.

Yet there is a deliberation implicit in the exercise, since by asking whether our society did or did not do what it ought to have, we determine how we are to act together now, clarifying the possibilities of action open to us. Are we to be penitent, or are we to advance triumphantly? Are we to atone for our guilt, or are we to demand reparations for our injuries? So it is more than an academic issue if Japanese schoolbooks are less than frank about Japan's role in the Second World War; while I am often impressed, on the other hand, by the German legislation, "illiberal" by all conventional standards, that makes it an offence to publish a denial of the historicity of the Holocaust. The practical justification for this severe restriction of academic freedom is that German citizens' future deliberations must be built on an unambiguous judgment on their past role. What is true for the history of our own societies is true also for other societies with which we deal. Politicians who exploit the past in the course of international polemics know very well the power of historical judgments to limit the freedom of adversaries' actions. Can anyone imagine, for instance, that the Western powers could have sustained policies toward Israel-Palestine that have long fostered terror and destruction on the ground and now threaten the whole stability of the West, without the constraint of a heavy burden of guilt?

In the second place, tradition is sustained through art,

whether visual, auditory, or performed. The peculiar value of art to tradition lies in its capacity to elicit recognitions, reminding us of the sources of our cultural objects within the structures of natural necessity. This power of reminiscence we call "beauty," and it arises from the coincidence of natural order with artificial form. Both poles, the natural and the conventional, are essential to an art form, that the evocation of the one within the other may be experienced. *Formal* qualities are as important as substantive references in evoking the presence of nature in culture. A poem may allude to springtime, or a tune may imitate birdsong. But an abstract fugue evokes nature, too, by exploiting the power of repetition in difference, and a sonnet by its balance of thesis, development, and resolution.

—⟋⟋—

But this whole depiction of how society uses transcendental representations trembles on the edge of a theological precipice. It proceeds entirely, as it were, on the premise of the state of innocence, and we can no longer defer the question what becomes of it when innocence is shattered.

To begin with, an obvious but ominous fact: there is more than one society, more than one set of social self-representations, and so more than one window on the world, each showing a somewhat different view. No sooner does a society recognize it-self through its representations than it recognizes others in com-petition with it. "Our signs," in the psalmist's terms, are over-whelmed by "their signs." This recognition creates an alarm much worse than any fear of competition for purely material goods. The very fact that competition in ideas is possible sets a question mark against the representations as such. The true pa-thos of the psalmist's lament, and the reason that his lament can become our own within the liturgy today, is the pathos of chal-lenged faith. It is not simply that the holy people of God has been overwhelmed, but that the self-conception of the "holy people of God" has been overwhelmed with it. Invited to sing "one of the songs of Zion" for his captors beside the waters of Babylon, an-other psalmist finds that the songs of Zion have no continuing tradition in that setting, and only cursing rises to his lips.[15]

The problem lies in an antinomy about the social media-tion of truth. Truth does not permit contradiction; but society does not permit unity. Yet if society is no longer *the* sphere and matrix of communication, it is not a sphere and matrix of true communication at all, and the whole conception of man as a social being collapses. Once the fact of plurality is confronted, societies find themselves in a self-contradictory posture. On

15. Psalm 137.

the one hand, there is a new urgency about maintaining tradition, since the very existence of other societies and their conflicting visions puts tradition at risk. On the other hand, the sense of urgency itself betrays the tradition, by admitting that it is not, as it pretends to be, a simple mediation of reality. For one cannot honestly relate to one's tradition like the conservator of a museum. It has to be lived in confidently.

Because of this antinomy the communication of tradition tends to be simultaneously urgent and yet dissimulated, as though the transmission of cultural knowledge were surrounded with a shame like the act of biological reproduction. This betrays an awareness that the tradition is fragile and imperfectible, at risk before the judgment of God in history and in truth. Modernity especially, born of a lively rediscovery of the relativity of traditions, concealed its own transmission of tradition by a tradition of scorn for tradition, so providing itself with a cloak to hide the nakedness of its self-perpetuation — like an enlightened schoolmaster who sets the pupils the discipline of writing out a hundred times the sentence, "Never reproduce what someone else has dictated!" This dissimulation finds decisive expression in the modern cleft between the descriptive sciences and normative philosophy — a cleft that runs down the middle of modern thought on society. By presenting the antinomies and contradictions of action as anthropological or historical descriptions, modern culture can give the impression of having taken due note of them, and proceed on its way as though it had somehow solved them. But this device leads it into its most characteristically modern extravagances. For as soon as we hand over the understanding of our social existence to the purely descriptive sciences and adopt the position of disinterested observers, we abandon the active hope that society may disclose a loving knowledge of the world to us. In which case we have no practical social philosophy available. We can only sink into despairing individualism, wringing our hands about what fools men are when they get together; or we can pretend to reinvent society from scratch on a sensible basis, as some kind of business contract.

Theology has had its own way of confronting this antinomy: a narrative that unfolds the fall and the redemption of society, its self-knowledge and its self-love. If the social mediation of the truth belongs to the state of innocence, may there not be, nevertheless, some hope for a redemption of it?

Let us look more closely first at this social and epistemological "fall." It is possible and tempting to think that it consists in the plural consciousness as such. Once we identify ourselves, we may say, as *this* society as opposed to *that*, all is lost. The self-positing of separate collectives with separate local identities generates the whole terrible history of intersocietal conflict. Innocence, then, must consist in the absence of all distinction between "us" and "them." Redemption must mean universal world-community without "barriers." In this proposal we can see a political version of the Neoplatonic thought of a fall from unity to plurality, and of sin as difference. The element of truth in it is that the conflict of signs is not merely a conflict over material goods, but a conflict of identities.

Yet it is not a Christian or Jewish view that sin is difference. Plurality is redeemable, and before the throne of God, John of Patmos tells us, stand a multitude of tribes and nations and peoples, no longer warring against one another, but still not absorbed into an indeterminate mass.[16] Plural self-consciousness is not itself the fall. One of the oldest reflections on plurality reversed the claim: the story of the Tower of Babel saw plurality as a necessary restraint, a curb on evil to which unity had given free rein.[17] The story of the primeval fall in Genesis presented the original temptation subtly: it was the "knowledge of good and evil," at once a discrimination to which human beings must come and a false pretension to achieve the perspective of God.[18] As the knowledge of good and evil was seized on before

16. Revelation 7:9-12 and passim.
17. Genesis 11:1-9.
18. Genesis 3:1-7.

it was granted, so a knowledge of distinct identity, too, can be come by too hastily. The sin that crouches at the door is idolatry: locking the transcendence of God into the structures of its own particularity. The society that forms a window through which its members see the world may become a screen which blocks out what is most worth seeing. "A man that looks on glass," George Herbert reminds us, "On it may stay his eye." The understanding that no political society can be entirely free of idolatry was Reinhold Niebuhr's most enduring insight.

The redemption of social knowledge must begin, then, with a moment of self-restraint, a patience that is prepared not to grasp. Israel learned that the holy, the coincidence of the social and cosmic, must in the end be waited for. Recall Ezekiel's great concluding vision of the holy, written in the wake of that desolation which the psalmist gave voice to. The foursquare temple is set at the center of the land, the palace united with the temple, the Holy Land has undergone massive geophysical changes, and the tribal territories are all redistributed around it. In one sense this vision is a renunciation. Ezekiel is heir not only to the priests who guarded the temple, but to the prophets who warned of the delusiveness of holy signs. No such holy land can be reentered now; no Cyrus will make it possible; no Ezra will legislate it into being. It can be cherished only as a promise, the promise of a new identity.

The Christian conception of the "secularity" of political society arose directly out of this Jewish wrestling with unfulfilled promise. Refusing, on the one hand, to give up what it knew of God, itself, and the world, accepting, on the other, that what it knew was incomplete and demanded validation, Israel understood itself and its knowledge and love of God as a contradiction to be endured in hope. "Secularity" is irreducibly an eschatological notion; it requires an eschatological faith to sustain it, a belief in a disclosure that is "not yet" but is absolutely presupposed as the inner meaning of what we know already. If we allow the "not yet" to slide toward "never," we say something entirely different and wholly incompatible, for the virtue that undergirds all secular politics is an expectant patience. What follows from the rejection of belief is an intolerable tension between the need for meaning in society and the only partial capacity of society to satisfy the need. An unbelieving society has forgotten how to be secular.

Let us explore this thought further by reflecting upon the need to secure an "identity." Persons are individual by virtue of the given individuality of their bodies, but identities are social, and societies have no natural individual bodies. There is, then, no necessity about the form and limits of one society over against another, and we must accept that our identities depend on something contingent and even conventional.

As I sit in my study in Oxford I enjoy the thought that I am only a few hundred yards away from an ancient international border, where the kingdoms of Wessex and Mercia once faced each other across the Thames. It was not *necessary*, merely historically convenient, that Wessex and Mercia should disappear into England, and England subsequently into Great Britain. Should some further historical convenience wrap Great Britain in turn into a unified European Nation, it will still not be a necessary development. Mercia, England, and in that case Great Britain will always be alternative possibilities, and perhaps nostalgic seductions. Thought is free to explore hypothetical other worlds, with no harm done. One may dream of an independent Mercia, as of Narnia; but to have a political identity means accepting the contingent determination of one's society by the decrees of God's historical providence, which allows no justification or criticism. Yet this is a difficult thing to accept, as modern nationalist movements constantly illustrate. It is always possible to imagine our society constituted differently, and always tempting to prefer the imagination to the reality.

"Which of the three, do you think, was neighbor to the man who fell among robbers?" Jesus asked.[19] The answer has

19. Luke 10:36.

implications that touch on the foundations of political society. It was not one who *chose* his neighbor, but one who *found* his neighbor on the road he traveled. The Good Samaritan exemplifies a kind of uncluttered common sense about community relations. He reacted to the simple fact of proximity. But such common sense is manifestly uncommon, since it requires a critical ascesis, stripping away the false social representations which constitute unreal but highly believable barriers. That ascesis is part of what is involved in the redemption of social knowledge.

But ascesis requires the disclosure of a universal society, a Kingdom of Heaven, a new identity capable of weaning us from dependence upon our varied identities. Without it we cannot envisage those identities in sober clarity, as grounds neither of boasting nor shame. Of course, the mere imagination of a universal society, as an ideal or a project, will not suffice for such an ascesis; for it can provide no real social identity, but only entangle us in a contested cause. We must become actual members of a real community constituted by the real and present image of God as uniquely lord, and the real and present image of mankind as subject uniquely to God. Jesus Christ, very God and very man, is the double representative around whom such a community has come into being.

3

A MULTITUDE OF RATIONAL
BEINGS UNITED

To pursue a critical ascesis in contemporary conditions we need some outline of an understanding of our own civilization, which requires what is often called "modernity-criticism." To discuss "modernity" is to ask about how life as human beings today is significantly different from what it was for earlier generations of humanity. "Significantly" is the important word, for the question assumes that not every alteration of our condition, not even of the more obvious ones, has a profound meaning. Paradoxically, therefore, a discussion of modernity starts from an assumption that there is general truth in the proverb *tout ça change, c'est la même chose.* We are all Adam's children, younger or older, and we all live under the eyes of Adam's creator. Were it not so, there could be no "modernity" as a development within history, for "history" would have been swallowed up by discontinuity and difference. There would only be "the world as we know it," on the one hand, and a kind of paleological deposit on the other, out of which it had emerged. Yet the point of modernity criticism is to examine how this general truth of human sameness seems to falter in the light of certain experiences, experiences which present us with peculiar moral difficulties, in which the task of being Adam's children seems to require something new of us, and we face a question about our human integrity. For Christian faith this question is related to a central theological one: how is creation vindicated in the coming of God's Kingdom? And how is the Kingdom seen to make creation new?

It is impossible for us not to confront that question somehow. We shall think about it either mythically or philosophically. The two great myths of modernity are those of progress and degeneration, and many people, perhaps most, simply adhere to one or the other of these, or to each in turn, depending on their shifting moods. Both imply that between modern humanity and what went before it the alteration has been qualitative: modern humanity is essentially the same, but either better or worse as such. A philosophical enquiry begins when we become discontented with these myths and begin to search for constitutive differences. This search has roots far back in modernity itself, arising at least as early as the early eighteenth century; but it gained pace through nineteenth-century reflections on history, and again in the twentieth century through philosophical reflections on technology.

Today, though it is a very recent development, modernity-criticism is a commonplace of the philosophical bazaar. It has even been claimed that the only possible form philosophy can take today is the critique of modernity.[20] But there is more than one way of proceeding with it. Some have thought to find the root of modernity in changed metaphysical assumptions, such as the Cartesian separation of *res extensa* from *res cogitans*, or in changed paradigms of practical thought, such as the contract theory of government, the utility theory of morality, or the notion of justice as human rights. Others have attended to the implications of freakish and innovative practices which set modernity at loggerheads with the universal moral consensus of the past: the systematic abortion of the human fetus, for example, or the practice of deterrence by threat of disproportionately massive destruction. And others still have sifted through the commonplaces, the different ways in which modern man-

20. Robert Spaemann, *Philosophische Essays,* 2nd ed. (Stuttgart: Philipp Reclam, 1994), p. 6: "So muss Philosophie heute explizit oder implizit Theorie der Moderne sein." "Radical Orthodoxy" might also be identified as making a parallel theological claim.

kind does the most simple and ordinary things. Here there has arisen the fruitful interest in technology, and also an important discussion of time; but I want to focus on a different theme, which is the distinctive character of modern communications in general, and in particular its representations. "Publicity" is the name we give to the most distinctively modern form of representation, a modern term (its origins in the eighteenth century) for a modern thing, which reached its full flowering more recently than that.

Let us begin our exploration from communication in words. That this is perilous was well understood by classical civilization. We may recall Virgil's commentary on rumor in Book 4 of the *Aeneid;* for another, no less searching, exploration of the waywardness of social truth we may refer to Herodotus's quizzical comparison of the beliefs and practices of different societies. But what were the options for defending communication against collective self-deception? The ancient world tried to solve the problem by socio-epistemic discipline: the location of responsibility for communication within a distinct social class with distinct rules of practice. The "wise man" of the ancient Near East was a determinative figure, the original "elite," whose role it was to correct the popular vision. He stood critically above the passions and misconceptions that dominated ordinary social intercourse. He was a standing resource for the prudent and ambitious, offering instruction in elementary criticism based on organized observation; and he was found especially close to the monarch's throne, for the connection between wisdom and the task of justice, as we find it in the biblical character of Solomon, was centrally important. But with the complexification of society the ancient world developed a second principle, that of socio-epistemic differentiation. Different forms of socially disciplined wisdom were to be called upon for different purposes: priestly, artistic, philosophical, legal, and so on.

A striking feature of this arrangement was the absence of anything that we would recognize as "news," i.e., a universal diffusion of information about universal happenings. Information, too, belonged within a specialist sphere, the sphere of government. It was the ruler's task to interest himself in what was going on beyond the local horizon, and messenger services were, not accidentally, the creation of empires. "As the eye is set in the body, so is the king in the world. . . . It brings distinction to the imperial power to have a comprehensive surveillance of its own, or to draw upon others', unashamedly acquiring knowledge and putting it to service promptly."[21] Ordinary

---

21. Agapetos *Heads of Advice* clauses 46 and 57. Translation in *From Irenaeus to Grotius: A Sourcebook in Christian Political Thought*, ed. O. O'Donovan & J. Lockwood O'Donovan (Grand Rapids: Eerdmans, 1999), pp. 186-87.

people did not need "news," just as they did not need a knowledge of religious ritual. Spheres of knowledge went hand in hand with spheres of responsibility; disciplined communication was ensured by disciplined social roles and responsibilities.

The general anxiety about the communication of truth was, if anything, even more strongly felt in ancient Israel. It gripped the prophetic movement of late seventh-century Judah and those whom it influenced, the royal administrators responsible for the great reform attempted in the Book of Deuteronomy. Anxiously aware of the inconsistencies and eclecticism of law and practice in the Israel of their day, disturbed by the threat it posed in the face of external pressures, they came to understand the process of oral tradition itself as a problem. Jeremiah dared to envisage a day when there would be no more oral tradition, when "no longer shall each man teach his neighbor and each his brother, saying 'Know the Lord,' for they shall all know me."[22] The Deuteronomists sought to discipline the process by determining it with a single authoritative and regulatory law-text, given in revelation and sustained in place by the watchful protection of a central sanctuary and a monarch. The authoritative text, however, allowed

22. Jeremiah 31:34.

Jews and, later, Christians to hang more loosely to socio-epistemic differentiation. The Deuteronomists could tell Israel that the authoritative word, which regulated and made possible all words, was very near them, in their mouths and in their hearts, needing no seer to receive a new disclosure from heaven, no foreign emissary to produce the latest report.

Following the logic of this, early Christianity took a radically egalitarian turn, cultivating a community in which all participated freely of the Spirit of God and had equal access to revelation through faith. "The Word was in the beginning with God. . . ." Recognize *that* Word on its coming into the world, and there can be no significant distinctions; for "to all who received him, who believed in his name, he gave power to become the children of God."[23] There was in the early church, of course, a role for a presbyterial priesthood in safeguarding the integrity of the gospel word against corrupt imaginations; and this was later to prove of decisive significance in providing a learned class to reconstruct the culture of Western Europe after the withdrawal of the Roman Empire. Yet the striking feature of Christian culture in the Western Middle Ages remained its homogeneity — that is to say, the interpenetration of the various branches of sacred and secular learning within an all-

23. John 1:2, 12.

encompassing word. That this did not have to be the case the rather different culture of Byzantium demonstrated. Only with the birth of modernity did the classical idea of differentiated learning revive itself vigorously in the West within the universities, giving its characteristic shape to academic life as we now know it.

Publicity stands in sharp contrast to this differentiated academic ideal. It reasserts homogenous culture; that is to say, one which differentiates neither the matter communicated nor the recipients. Mass man, negatively defined by the lack of special calling and spiritual vocation, transmits a confused mix of news, advertising, and entertainment, a populism that may be seen as a late fruit of the Pentecostal inspiration in Christianity. But that poses the question: what prospect can there be for a Pentecostal discourse that depends on no Holy Spirit and acknowledges no gospel? Is this not another instance of theological hope recast in a secular mold that cannot sustain it? What can stand between this communication and the self-destructive dominion of rumor? The air of unreality surrounding the "Diana phenomenon" illustrated the extent to which reality and projection become indistinguishable to a media-formed society.

"In the beginning was the Word . . ." says the prologue of St. John's Gospel, establishing, in a world where there are words aplenty, that there is such a thing as *the* Word, the normative word, which was in the beginning with God. But when "the Word became flesh . . . we beheld his glory." We have, therefore, to recognize a visual image also. This image is not autonomous and self-replicating. It is the *particular* image brought to being by the Word in becoming flesh.

The attitude of YHWH, the God of Israel, to images of the divine is well known. God is to be known by word alone, not by visual representation, since depiction can only project onto the divine the self-replication of creaturely artifice. The word is not artifice, but is the element, abyssal and self-sustaining, into which the creature is called by the Creator. This refusal of the image is reproduced in the political theology of Israel, resistant as it was even to the idea of monarchy. The right of government belonged to God, and YHWH would be his people's only king. If the throne of David could be understood as a condescension to the people's weakness, the throne of Jeroboam quite definitely could not. For the tribes of Jacob had chosen Jeroboam for themselves and this was to place an image in the seat of God. The crimes of rebellion and idolatry seemed to Israel to be one and the same.

The early church still regarded political representation as essentially rebellious; the angels, principalities, and powers that embodied the governments of the nations had to be disarmed, humbled, and overthrown by the cross of Christ. To this view corresponds Saint Paul's famous passage on the role of government in Romans 13, in which the whole question of the representative status of government is passed by in silence and its rationale is found exclusively in the tasks of justice. Government is to enact God's word of judgment; that and nothing else. The desire to have a government in one's image is like the desire to have God in one's image. John of the Apocalypse, finally, renews the conception that false government is idolatrous. His anti-Christ sets up an image that his "false prophet" (the Third Person of his diabolical anti-Trinity) commands people to worship. The word in the service of an image is an overturning of all true relations.

There was a point in Christian history at which Christian culture took a decisive stance in relation to visual representational ascesis; and this occurred, intriguingly enough, against the backdrop of the nascent Islamic culture of the Middle East. This was the iconoclastic controversy of the eighth and ninth centuries, which concerned the proposition that visual representations of Christ should have no part in Christian worship. The undoubted strength of the iconoclastic position was its radical appeal to the prohibition of three-dimensional art in ancient Israel, expressed in the second command of the Decalogue. In response to this appeal the anti-iconoclastic Orthodox pointed to the prologue of St. John's Gospel, with its claim to have seen the glory of the incarnate word, and to St. Paul's claim that the Galatians had seen Christ publicly portrayed as crucified before their eyes.[24] To abolish visual images, they argued, would be to fall back from that decisive moment in salvation history, at which the divine presence made itself available to the visual sense.

What was required, rather, was the correct *situation* of icons within the ministry of the gospel word. "We depict Christ as king and lord," wrote John of Damascus from the heart of Muslim-dominated territory, "without stripping him of his array."[25] His "array" was the visibility of his rule, its availability to faith through sensual signs, which formed the basis of the community of faith and hope. This licensed artistic depictions of Christ, but also kept them in a subordinate place, since the actual image, the face and form that the apostles saw, will be known to us only at the second coming. Icons were "memorials," testimonies that the incarnation happened, and could never be undone. Christian art was free, but humble, an object of respect, but not of worship; for it was a creature and servant of the apostolic word.

It is notable how this response broadens the question from

24. John 1:14; Galatians 3:1.
25. *On Images* 2.5.

its narrow focus on visual art to include every aspect of the representation of the being and works of God. Yet it remains keenly on guard against the *autonomous* projection of images, determined to establish an iconic discipline proper to the gospel era. The iconoclastic emperors themselves, it argued, merely hoped to replace the visible icons of Christ the King with the sensible array of their own imperial state, so intruding themselves in Christ's place as God's representatives on earth. Dispensing with all representation was not a possibility for the church of the incarnation, but neither was undisciplined representational chaos. The prohibition of images in Israel was a discipline proper to the age of law, which included the early disapproval of kingship, since a God unrepresentable by images could not be represented by monarchs either. But these restraints were only the negative aspect of a positive focus upon holy images in Israel's life: the city of Jerusalem, the temple, and, one should add, prophetic action and oracle itself. These in their turn had to be transcended in the fullness of time, so that all representation came to a rest in the living image of the invisible God, Jesus Christ himself. The issue for Christian society, then, was how *that* image could be faithfully displayed at the center of a living community. Today, looking back on that controversy from a huge spiritual distance and from the heart of a culture where the proliferation of images is uncontrolled, the very idea of iconic discipline may seem incomprehensible. So it is possible to miss the whole significance of the victory over iconoclasm, which was not to *refuse* the Jewish discipline, but to establish an evangelical discipline that corresponded to it, focusing attention upon the revealed Savior of the world.

In the light of this controversy the events of last September 11 begin to assume a certain intelligibility. To understand the furious, sacrificial, and resolute hostility directed against the West it is not enough to echo politicians' rhetoric about "enemies of democracy and civilization," which is the language of pure bafflement. Underlying these events is a much wider conflict between a religious culture identified with the iconoclastic proposition, and a culture marked not by an evangelical discipline but by publicity, the profuse proliferation of communicated images of every kind. These two cultures, rooted originally in the two world religions that proclaimed the universal reign of God on earth, sprang up in recent times from what had seemed on both sides to be a comfortable and stable accommodation with secularity in a plural nation-state system; but both have now leaped across the borders of political organization, and radicalized their universalizing tendencies.

—◊—

Publicity is not the same as being or acting in public, which is fundamental to every form of political life. Being and acting in public — what Hannah Arendt has influentially expounded as "appearing" — is *reciprocal;* the public is a realm of action in which we are accountable to one another without familiarity.[26] A day at the office filling in forms and writing reports is the archetypal public existence of our time, the way in which each of us "appears" before the nonfamiliar community to which we are accountable and through which we hold others accountable. Publicity, on the other hand, is nonreciprocal. In this respect it is more like what was traditionally called "glory" or "fame." Like those, publicity is a kind of universal gaze. But unlike fame, it selects its subjects with apparent arbitrariness, irrespective of what they have achieved, and unlike glory, it selects them without reference to the public institutions in which they shine. The visibility given by publicity is neither the radiance of accomplishment nor the floodlighting of major social institutions. It is a roaming spotlight, catching people unpredictably in its beam. It does not accrue to projects, planning, virtues of performance, teamwork, durable results, or anything of merit. It is interested only in those moments over

26. See especially the opening chapter of *The Life of the Mind* (New York: Harcourt Brace, 1981), and pp. 38-60 in the unpublished Oxford doctoral thesis of T. E. Breidenthal, "The Concept of Freedom in Hannah Arendt" (1991).

which its subjects have little or no control: their spontaneous reactions or their embattled struggles. Publicity is attracted not by achievement, but by pathos.

Publicity assigns the possibility of recognition to names and faces; but it does so not for the benefit of those who have *practical* business with those names and faces, but for the benefit of a public essentially indifferent to them. It evokes recognition from those who have no apparent interest in recognizing. And this feature is what betrays its role as a device of social coherence. The business of publicity is *creating* common interests, *generating* common representations. One could say that it imposes recognition as a kind of civic discipline. To know the names of those in the public eye — footballers, let us say, or pop stars — is a proof of social competence.

Yet nobody and nothing directs the roaming spotlight of publicity. The all-powerful press baron — as much an imaginary construction of the age as the all-powerful president — is paradoxically the creature of the process he is supposed to control, the arbitrariness of publicity itself. I do not mean, of course, that journalists have no freedom of decision, or no moral responsibility for what they publicize. I mean simply that, like fishermen, who are masters of the harvest of the sea only as they become the servants of its tides and its humors, so those who gather in the fruits of publicity are treating with something like a natural force. They exert control to the extent that they accommodate to its conditions.

Publicity is never neutral; it is always "good publicity" or "bad publicity." That is to say, the recognitions it imposes are part of a system of judgments; they are society's favorable and unfavorable verdicts. These verdicts demand only soft assent, for a humane liberal society allows dissent its own dignity. One who refuses to agree with them is not thrown into jail, merely looked upon as odd or unreliable. Yet the demand for acquiescence, though soft, is so encompassing and so persistent that it may seem to achieve by stifling insistence something of the same oppressiveness that other forms of social imposition achieve by brutality.

In singling out its objects for negative and positive recognition, publicity presents them selectively and interpretatively. They are assigned representative roles, they stand for something that society conceives itself, complacently or anxiously, as containing. They thus become an element in society's own self-representation. Publicity homogenizes events and people. Throughout the republic of publicity, platitude and cliché hold sway, building and reinforcing stereotypical forms that are easy to recognize. The concern of publicity is not with individual agents and events at all, but with typical characterizations. Individuality is ironed out and unique characteristics suppressed; for the purposes of public representation, everyone must be the instance of a type. The whole project is, one may say, that of overcoming the unknown, closing off the genuinely open, taking the threat out of untold and unrealized purposes by associating each new name with a pathos that is predictable, familiar, and, to use the favorite word of the publicist, "human." If one appears in the public eye, one appears *as* something, and something rather well-known: an old fuddy-duddy, a brave knight-errant, a whacky jester, a heartless administrator, an angel of compassion. That something is not what one *determined* to be, but simply one of a number of fixed roles, which society has at its disposal for self-imaging, like costumes in a theater company's wardrobe, and which it likes to have represented to it often. The gratification of being the object of attention is the bait with which society allures prominent individuals into accepting these prescribed roles. Publicized, one is not the master of one's own appearing. So there is a wisdom in avoiding publicity, a wisdom not confined to criminals or conspirators, who have something to hide, but well known to anyone with serious business to accomplish.

The media of publicity embrace at least three different undertakings: news, advertising, and entertainment. The official theory is that these three are quite distinct. The news does positive social good, producing an "informed public"; advertising pays for the provision of news; and entertainment wins an audience for it. In reality the three enterprises are more homogeneous and more closely interwoven than the official doctrine allows. Each imposes recognitions, and the proportionately tiny amount of media output devoted to news can only suggest that in modern society other recognitions are of equal importance. Seepage constantly occurs among the three enterprises, hardly resisted. I note that the Shorter Oxford English Dictionary includes the neologism "infomercial" with a disapproving definition that attributes the term to North America, while the parallel neologism "infotainment," with an evaluatively neutral definition, is allowed to be British English. In a recent example of British television infotainment, prominent people were induced into giving interviews in the belief that they were participating in a serious news documentary, when in fact they were part of an entertainment "spoof." No serious criticism was made of this procedure by the servile body, misnamed an Authority, which rules on television matters in Great Britain. It observed only that the subject of this merriment, which was child abuse and child murder, should have been notified to the public beforehand. The program-makers defended their enterprise with the argument, easy to believe (alas!), that it was at least as serious-minded as a real news documentary.

Advertising is a form of communication entirely created within the sphere of modern publicity; and we can see it as a protected enclave in which the rule that nobody directs communications is suspended. It expresses a limit-possibility, at once the goal and the sublimation of publicity, desired and feared in equal measure: that some human beings should control what others communicate. The nuclear core of direct control is ceremoniously, if ineffectively, protected from seepage by being confined within the boundaries of a purely commercial transaction. Yet it has never been clear that a strictly *commercial* rationale for advertising exists. The necessity for advertising is less a commercial and more a sociological one: commerce is so close to the heart of what we take society to be that it must be represented in our communications. Business wears advertising as Peers wear ermine, not to accomplish anything but to maintain its dignity.

The third strand in the chord is entertainment, and here the situation is quite different.

The media have digested forms of communication traditionally sustained elsewhere: on the stage, in concert halls, in drawing rooms, and on sports fields. Their value to the modern project is their morally communicative function.

Seepage between news and entertainment is continual and

hardly resisted. Indeed, anything that happens in a sufficiently prominent sport or soap opera *is* news.

These older forms of communication do not remain unchanged by their absorption into the media. Drama, which is of particular importance as morality, has been reinforced in the visual media by making the images of actors and actresses permanent. Many actors have been Hamlet on the stage, but only Dirk Bogarde is Gustav von Aschenbach on the screen. Visconti will do more than Shakespeare to shape the moral recognitions of our age.

Is publicity really new? From one point of view it is simply the way in which certain sociological universals are manifest in modern society. We form a community by communication, and especially by communicated understandings. And by means of special representations a society reflects upon itself, and invests its leaders with representative legitimacy. The Emperor Justinian bolstered his authority by being seen at popular sporting occasions, backing his favorite team; and our own politicians do the same.

Yet we must observe at least that modern communications have assumed a fevered pace, and the generation of social symbols has gone into overdrive. There is an apparent surplus of representative identifications — too great an excess to be explained by the ordinary needs of political legitimation. And they change with mercurial speed, too quickly to serve the purposes of social coherence or stability. To which we should add that one feature of late-modern communications is wholly distinctive: its dependence upon the visual-erotic. The portrayal of the naked human form in all possible shapes, textures, motions, and combinations predominates in our communications in a way that no previous civilization has ever anticipated. It is often said that the sexual *mores* of our times are unprecedented, and this may or may not be true. But it is a separate point, and no less important, that it makes unprecedented use of the erotic image. Inescapably symbolic, the erotic image is capable of securing immediate and irresistible engagement of the viewer's attention, and so serves the purposes of publicity with immediate effect, locating the viewer unarguably *vis à vis* some typical scene with typical actors. The visual-erotic is, as it were, the stamp of authority, which commands us to engage with society's self-representation.

Our first exploratory speculation about this phenomenon as a whole must surely be that it looks like an attempt to compensate for the loss of something. It would seem that modern society perceives itself as affected by a kind of social numbness, an incapacity to receive and respond, which demands a hectoring and overheated style of communications as an antidote. The feverish generation of words and images indicates the disappearance of certain stable and solid points of ideological reference that an earlier society could count on. The intense reinforcement of simple stereotypes is a response to a crisis of social representation. Where could the underlying loss be situated?

First, modern society has carried to extraordinary lengths the specialization of social functions. Communication is threatened by a diversity of competencies that makes each part of the social organism comparatively inaccessible to other parts. Space for action in the public realm is found, as it were, only in crevices or on narrow ledges of society. Everywhere else is the domain of specialisms, which are the aristocracies of our age.

Second, having abandoned a realist conception of moral relations, society is in need of a mechanism to impose judgments that it can no longer argue for on the basis of the moral law. We have commented on the moralism of publicity, its persistent reinforcement of negative and positive stereotypes; and in this respect it takes over roles traditionally associated with moral and religious education, but replaces stable categories and laws to be applied in free decision, with normative narratives to be related and imitated.

Third, it provides the legitimation required by the evolution of democratic political forms and populist ideologies. Officeholders do not remain in office long and are not selected for office by any fixed rule, so that the task of securing legitimacy for them is much greater. Like giant pandas, always eating to keep alive, and so knowing no difference between acquiring and expending energy, the insatiable electoral mouth of the body politic requires a proliferation of communicated symbols. So, too, does the degeneration of democratic theory into naive populism. The illusion that rulers can be seen not as representatives but as delegates of the people can be sustained only by unremitting legitimating exercises of publicity. Which means that representation itself becomes the dominant issue of modern politics, and displaces the true goal of political structures, which is the enactment of justice.

But besides compensating for loss, the phenomenon of publicity mediates certain distinctive *persuasions* of a society that has departed from the philosophical beliefs of its ancestors. It mediates, first, the conviction that the identity of any thing lies in change. The rejection of fixed essences has as its corollary that our knowledge of the world must constantly be kept up-to-date. It cannot be known as it is, only as it is becoming, each new day's communications making the previous day's obsolete. Publicity mediates change by putting the work of symbolic representation in narrative form. Here lies the special nuance of the word "information" (in its general, not its technical, sense): information, unlike knowledge, supersedes itself continually; it excludes philosophical utterances, and it substitutes for history in a society that understands itself as constructing its own history.

Second, and for our purposes most importantly, publicity mediates universalism, the aspiration to overcome differences and unify communications within a single world-communicative sphere. Modernity began its career with three centuries of conquest-colonialism; but after that had exhausted itself, the universalizing tendency found a new home in communications. The possibility of globally transmitted visual images spearheaded an expansive movement, which, bypassing obstacles posed by differences of language, placed Western images on cinema and TV screens throughout the globe. Then, in the most intense and naive way, the coming of the Internet renewed talk of overcoming boundaries, with many of its early advocates explicitly commending it as a means of bypassing national political control. It is hardly surprising if these anarchistic aspirations, easily underestimated by Western observers, appeared in other parts of the globe as a serious declaration of colonial intent. It is difficult not to see the revival of radical Islamism as a direct reaction to the universal ambitions of Western communications, "international terrorism" as the mirror image of the dream of the founders of the Internet, a

way of imposing universal representation. In this universalizing thrust we may observe how Western society has forgotten
how to be secular. Secularity is a stance of patience in the face
of plurality, made sense of by eschatological hope; forgetfulness of it is part and parcel with the forgetfulness of Christian
suppositions about history.

Political theology of the twentieth century shadowed the
wider preoccupation of the century with the dangers of authoritarian regimes and the role of political ideology as a tool
of oppression. In doing so it called, with good reason, on the
New Testament testimonies to which I have alluded, i.e., the
passages about the defeat of the principalities and powers and
the critique of ideological empire in the Apocalypse. Yet it
failed to notice that it is *political representation* against which
the critique of these texts is directed. It conceived the problem
of political authority entirely quantitatively, supposing that
authoritarianism was excess of authority and the cure must either be an Aristotelian moderation or a liberal minimalism.
This led it mistakenly to throw in its lot with populist suspicion of authority, and so it fell into a trap; for this proceeds, as
we have seen, precisely by *enhancing* the importance of representation within government.

Authoritarianism, especially of the ideological kind,
springs not from excess of authority, but from a perversion of

it, which fails to receive it from its source in the true word of judgment, from outside and prior to all existing society, and attempts to construct it instead upon the self-projection of society. The critique of authoritarianism ought to extend not into a critique of authority, but into a critique of social self-projection. It is, in fact, precisely as governments conceive themselves as an image, expressing a soul, or personality, or ideals of a people, that they overreach themselves and depart from the terms of their mandate for justice. The sociological thrust to self-imaging, then, is the root problem, whether expressed in authoritarian forms, or, as in late-modern liberal society, in intensified forms of communication. If theology in liberal society simply joins the liberal hue and cry against conspiracies of power-holders it evades the real critique by displacing it. The media are not the product of a conspiracy. They are the sign of the universal corruptibility of man's communications, of which theology has always known.

At the beginning of the Christian era John of Patmos knew already that the appearance of the universal kingdom must call forth a false universal, an image that would lay immediate claim upon the world's loyalty. In closing, we should heed what John urged in the face of it: alertness, patience, and worship. Alertness, because believers are threatened with loss of their identity: "Blessed is he who is awake, keeping his garments, that he may not go naked and be seen exposed."[27] That it might be stripped of its true representation, overwhelmed by the alien image, is a danger which the church must at all times take seriously, especially when it is in an exploratory mood, seeking, quite properly, appropriate cultural *entrées* for the commendation of the gospel. There is a "call for patience," too, because an iconic discipline means conflict, the burden of which has to be sustained, not evaded.[28] By refusing to escape it or to adjust the terms on which it arises, the church proves and displays the strength of its own common object of love.

These two apparently quietist dispositions were envisaged by John as means of conquest. That is because they are disciplines of attention, focusing upon the one representation that alone sustains a community of resistance. In his prophecy the community is seen only in worship, united before the throne of heaven with saints and martyrs of all ages, praising God's judgments that have been revealed. It has no other form of presence or service. Worship is the true posture of the represented, allowing the one representative image to rule all other images. Yet that one is not without its reflections; for the worshippers themselves bear a sign upon their forehead, as do the

27. Revelation 16:15.
28. Revelation 14:12.

71

worshippers of the false image, too. There is a visible sign of the Kingdom of God in the community that waits upon it. Its apparent passivity is an active power in the designs of saving providence. Not by creating images, but by being itself a true reflecting image, it serves the victory of the representative.

Christ our passover has been sacrificed for us;
therefore let us celebrate the feast.[29]

29. 1 Corinthians 5:7-8.